Christ the Yard

Christ the Yard

A Guide to Christian Living and Ministry
on the College Campus

MARCUS M. JONES

RESOURCE *Publications* • Eugene, Oregon

CHRIST THE YARD
A Guide to Christian Living and Ministry on the College Campus

Resource Publications
An Imprint of Wipf and Stock Publishers
199 W. 8th Ave., Suite 3
Eugene, OR 97401

www.wipfandstock.com

PAPERBACK ISBN: 978-1-5326-1683-9
HARDCOVER ISBN: 978-1-4982-4078-9
EBOOK ISBN: 978-1-4982-4077-2

Manufactured in the U.S.A.   JUNE 27, 2017

To the Brothers of Fellowship:
Terrence, Will, Thomas, and Jarrett.
Brothers in Christ, brothers for life.
This book is possible because of you . . .

And Rev. Brewington!

People value authenticity, affection, and action.

MARCUS JONES

Contents

Preface

The college experience is truly what a person makes it to be. It can be the best of times, or it can be the worst of times. This is especially true for the student who is a Christian. Students often begin college through the lens of their parents: They pick majors their parents would approve, they worship in the fashion they would if still living with parents, and they even view God and the world through their parents' eyes. It's not until the freedom that college brings that they see things for themselves that change those ideals. The purpose of this book is to serve as a guide to help Christians in college create experiences unique to how God desires them to grow and engage others. Let the Spirit guide you!

Preface

Acknowledgments

There is no *Christ the Yard* without Jesus Christ, revealed to a wayward young boy from Dallas and transformed his life the Yard of Huston-Tillotson University. Thank you, Jesus, for meeting me on the Yard and changing my life. To my beautiful wife, Tiffany. This book is possible because of your unending support of my career. God truly favors me, and I know it each time I look at you. To my sons, Jalen and Ian, who have spent more time on a college campus than most kids your age. Thank you for sharing your father with so many students. I love you. Lastly, to Huston-Tillotson University. The Yard that cultivated so much of who I am, and who I am to become. Thank you for giving me a place to serve in ministry as a student and minister. You are my fRAMily for life!

Introduction

Before you begin reading this book, the title may gen-
erate a few questions that are swirling around in your
brain. "What is the Yard?", "What does Christ have to do
with it?", and "Why does anyone want to Christ the Yard?"
Well, the "Yard" is a term that refers to a place where people
meet, connect, and fellowship that is typically in an open
area surrounded by several buildings. Places that typically
are considered yards are places that create space for different groups of people to come together for a common purpose, goal, or occasion. Specifically, the term yard is likely
to be used on the campuses of Historically Black Colleges
and Universities (HBCUs), but not exclusively. "Yard", as
reference to the college campus, was popularized by the
2007 film *Stomp the Yard* starting actors Columbus Short
and Meagan Good.[1] The term "yard" has many uses, including but not limited to, the "front/back yard", "prison yard",
referring to the space where incarcerated persons gather
during times of recess, or idioms such as "the whole nine

1. Good, Meagan; Short, Columbus. *Christ the Yard*. DVD. Di-
rected by Sylvain White. Atlanta, Columbia:2007

yards", indicating the full extent of something. The term as it is used on the college campus is the basis for this book, and will guide the discussion on engaging in meaningful Christian ministry and social interactions.

In the early years of Christianity, there was a common belief among critics and non-believers of the faith that the primary adherents were unintelligent, illiterate, and some of the least educated in society.[2] While it is relatively true that many of the early Christians were common civilians with little to no formal education, the movement would not have been able spread as rapidly without the assistance of some benefactors who perhaps were educated and/or wealthy (Romans 16:1-2), and others who able to utilize the skill of writing for Paul and the other apostles and disciples.

The relationship between Christianity and the Yard has a long, rich history. Many of the great Christian movements began in the halls of libraries and universities. John Wesley, the founder of Methodism, gathered together with a group of men on the Yard of Oxford University in England, where they were first called "Methodist" for their methods of consistent prayer, bible studies, and sharing of God's Word.[3] Later, many of the colleges and universities in the United States of America would be founded by mainline Christian denominations and other Christian groups. Unfortunately, however, some of these institutions, with rich histories of Christian activism, evangelism, and scholarship, currently have little to no resemblance of that history.

Each year on Yards across America, hundreds upon thousands of students enroll with an array of plans for the new life they shall embark upon. For some, the desire is to get

2. Wayne Meeks, *The First Urban Christians: The Social World of the Apostle Paul*, 51.

3. Richard P. Heitzenrater. *Wesley and The People Called Methodist*, 35

ahead of the academic rat race, excel in classes with anticipation to graduate early or within four years, and ultimately land that great job that will build their dream life. For others, it is to party, explore the pool of dating, and enjoy all the extracurricular activities that come with college life. Still others may desire to become a part of an organization like a fraternity or sorority. Yet sprinkled amongst the mass of students seeking the knowledge and direction that will prepare them to operate in various vocations, there are students searching for a deeper understanding of self, to live for a greater purpose, and discovering an overwhelming desire to respond to a destiny far beyond the degree they will obtain at the end of collegiate matriculation. There is an inner tugging to live life to the fullest, and to give life to others; a yearning to empower and encourage beyond the limitation of the systems of society, and display a character that audibly draws others to the same. These students have or yearn for a relationship with Jesus Christ, and perhaps even desire to share their yearnings with others. These students are the reason for this book.

This book was written for the students who may feel isolated in an environment that appears to be governed by sex, drinking, drugs and parties. It is for the ministry groups who actively desire to guide their peers into a relationship with Christ but feel ineffective in their approach. This book is for students who are Christian, and would like to learn how to be steadfast in their public devotion for Christ but are fearful of rejection, slander, and abandonment. This book will serve as a guide to passionate individuals with a heart for God's people in a place where God seems to be in last place in the race of life. By the end of this book, and prayerfully as each page is read, ideas will be created, confidence will be established, and wisdom will be received to become consistently courageous and Christian. Let's Christ the Yard!

Chapter One

"The Interest Meeting" (Informational)

Among the hundreds of thousands of institutions of higher learning in the world, one school that stands out most vividly when thinking about the activity of the Yard is the University of Texas in Austin, a prestigious institution known for its greatness in research and academics. The school is also known for their National Championship Football program, producing professional and Hall of Fame athletes and coaches such as legendary coach Tom Landry, Hall of Fame running back Earl Campbell, Seattle Seahawks safety Earl Thomas, former Tennessee Titans quarterback Vince Young, and the list continues. The University of Texas has produced graduates that would later help change the nation such as Senator Kay Bailey Hutchinson, Former First Ladies Laura Bush (wife of President George W. Bush) and Lady Bird Johnson (wife of President Lyndon B. Johnson) and former Texas Governor Ann Richards. Like movies? Graduates Matthew McConaughey and Owen Wilson star in them. Every aspect of society, from government officials to Hollywood celebrities have graced the University of Texas' campus as a student. One of the most compelling reasons to attend UT (not to be confused with University of Tennessee, as understand this is a conflict of interest for students of that institution), however, is its location.

Austin, Texas is a college student dream location, with over 100,000 students attending institutions of higher learning within the metropolis area, including UT. Austin considers itself "The Live Music Capital of the World"[1] College students parade the Historic Sixth Street, a busy, bar and club littered street in Downtown Austin, where live music can be heard Monday through Sunday, almost 365 days a year. Yet this even fails in comparison to South by Southwest (SXSW), a two-week festival of interactive film, live music of every genre, and other forms of art that literally bring millions of dollars to the city every March. This kind of atmosphere is conducive to a "student-gone-wild" lifestyle. And even with all this activity happening around the University of Texas at Austin, one of the most striking occurrences a student can experience on its Yard, like other colleges around the country, is the invitation to be a part of something greater than oneself. Campuses are lined and filled with posters, bulletin boards, signs, banners, and students from every organization under the auspice of the institution soliciting new comers to join their group for the purposes that it serves. Before the student is settled into their dorm, they have been bombarded with more information and choices than a college athlete attempting to turn pro! The main purpose of these beginning of the year solicitations by organizations and groups are to create a buzz that will increase the chances of their member intake.

Membership intake among college organizations are intentional and well planned. Organizations spend adequate amounts of time preparing to advertise and target

1. Mose Buchele. *"How Did Austin Become the Live Music Capital of the World"*, Sept. 21, 2016.

students they believe are a fit for their organization. The bylaws, principles, guidelines, rules, and history are reexamined and prepared for potential candidates.

In the book of Acts, the disciples prepare for membership intake in similar ways after Jesus' ascension into heaven. They continued in fellowship, studied the teachings of the disciples, and shared all things together.[2] Christians on the Yard need to do all we can to increase our Kingdom "membership" in-take. We should be looking to create opportunities for others to see what we are all about, gain a snap shot of our "Organization", to *determine* that following Jesus is the "Way, Truth and Life!"(John 14:6) We need to have an "Interest Meeting". Interest meetings are formal, yet discrete gatherings to determine who has interest in becoming a member of the organization. In Greek letter organizations, meetings are typically an open invitation, allowing students to gather surface information about the organization, while being unknowingly screened by the leaders to determine the right "fits". In the body of Christ, our interest meetings are a tad bit different. Our goal is to create the largest, most effective organization on the campus. We introduce our "Founders" (Father, Son, and Holy Spirit) up front; we do not interview candidates because all who come can join. We share our bylaws (Bible), discuss our mission and vision (grow in knowledge of Christ and equip one another to create disciples), and even allow them to partake in our extracurricular activities (church, small groups and discussions, fellowships). This creates an excitement about Jesus that transcends throughout the campus, having other organizations curious about what we are doing. All this comes from simply sharing information.

At the end of our interest meetings, students should be able to identify if following Jesus is a decision they would

2. Acts 2:41–42

like to make, and the necessary steps to living a life as a faithful, servant leader. We also have to be aware, just as other organizations and groups experience, not everyone invited to the informational will want to join. This shouldn't discourage you, even though sometimes it will seem as if the person is insane not to follow Jesus after you speak to them. Remember, a passage in Proverbs states" all the ways of a man are clean in his own sight, but the LORD weighs the motives" (Proverbs 16:2 NASB). It is not for us to judge or criticize people for their choice to not to follow Jesus, or subscribe to our view of God. This will help us in our approach, remaining aware that we too have been redeemed from our own sight that was led by the same *unconscious* motives. In the coming chapters, we will discuss methods and ways to reach even the most religiously dissatisfied students.

Now if you are student who yearns to 1) connect with the Christian organizations on your campus, 2) to find other Christians to hang out with, or 3) you have just begun to follow Christ, it also becomes your responsibility to seek and connect with others. Luke 11:9 records, " . . . ask, and it will be given to you; seek, and you will find; knock, and it will be opened to you." It is extremely easy, especially as a young Christian in a new environment, to take the shy role and remain alone until someone welcomes you into their circle. The fellowship, security, and growth that comes from being connected with other Christians will be lifesaving . . . literally. Taking the shy role, or remaining alone can open the door to opportunities to do things that will keep you away from God and other Christians. Let me be the first to say to you . . . Pray for courage, wisdom, and resilience (I will explain why these attributes are so important in the next chapter), then make yourself known to others as a follower of Christ! Some of you may be introverts (individuals who are more reserved and need some collective time to open up) and that is fine. Just remember that college life and its activities will surround a student quickly, and if you are alone (as to say without like-minded peers), you will experience a plethora of choices that can distract you spiritually, academically, and socially. When students are unaware of the spiritual detriments that are attached to life on the Yard, some will begin to struggle with academics and social relationships as the year matriculates. Students will become entangled with the "lit" activities of college, which can lead to laziness, poor class attendance, and bad grades that may cause them to drop out of school or choose a lifestyle that doesn't resemble a Christian. At times you may feel like there is no reason to live for Christ, or seek participation of a Christian organization because of students who "confess" to follow Jesus yet follow the popular trends . . . even among Christian leaders! Try not to let this be an excuse for you because your responsibility as a Christian is greater than the actions of others. In the next chapter, I help you see the benefits to following, serving, and exemplifying Christ on the campus, even if no one else is doing it!

INTEREST QUESTIONS

1. If you are a Christian, what values do you look for in Christian fellowship and organization?

2. Are you seeking healthy Christian fellowship or are you a Christian that would rather be alone?

3. Is there information readily available to help students know where to connect with your ministries and/or groups?

4. What does your organization do that will stand out from other organizations?

5. Write down some ideas that come to mind after reading this chapter that will make your college experience and organization appealing to others.

REFLECTION SCRIPTURES

- John 14:6
- Proverbs 16:2
- Luke 11:9
- 2 Timothy 2:22

Chapter Two

"If No One Comes?"

There is nothing like planning a birthday party, sending out invitations, buying cake and ice cream, and no one shows up. That's how it feels sometimes as a Christian in this modern world. This truth is even more evident on college campuses. The Yard isn't always set up to support the lifestyle of Christians and the people are not always going in the direction of Christ. But if it were different, Jesus would have been inaccurate in His statement in Matthew 7:14 "Because narrow is the gate and difficult is the way, there are few who find it". This scripture reminds me of an experience one of my mentors once told me about one of his campus ministry events years ago.

In 2000, while serving as a campus leader, one of my mentors, Pastor Corey Tabor of Full Life Community Church in Austin, was planning a conference on the campus of the University of Texas. He had prepared to teach an eight hour conference to about forty-five people, printed and put together material for each anticipated person, and even ordered lunches from Jason's Deli that would accommodate them all. On the day of the conference, there was an amazing four person attendance-Corey, his wife, and two others! What was Pastor Corey's response? He taught the conference as if everyone he anticipated had come, and enjoyed the unused sandwich lunches for the remainder of the week. His attitude was simple, "If Jesus will leave 99 to search for one surely I can teach 3 and be happy about it!" This should be our attitude to serve on our respective Yards. Yes it gets difficult, but the reward of doing the work of Christ will be the push we need to keep going. What should an organization do when situations such as this occur? Simply do it again. Christians and campus ministry organizations should see every opportunity to win someone to Christ as a success, whether it's one person or one hundred.

The number one way to become discouraged when doing the work that we believe is a benefit to God, is to fail to meet expectations. This is not to say having goals and expectations are a bad thing; however, Christ's standard for success is not the same as the world's standard. When we fail to reach our expected number of participants for an event or accomplish a certain task as planned, our first mental inclination is "I guess it wasn't meant to happen that way!" And we are exactly right; it wasn't supposed to happen that way. Proverbs 19:21 states "Many are the plans of man's heart, but it is the Lord's purpose that prevails" (NIV). In other words, we will have many plans and expectations but only what God intents to happen will happen. The Bible has many examples that show how we are to be faithful to do our part and allow God to do His part. This is the truth and hope that will allow us to be satisfied with what we do for Christ on our campuses.

For some, like Pastor Corey, the attitude of "next time will be better" will be easy to adapt and keep good heart in the pursuit to sharing the love of Christ and helping people get to know Jesus; for others not so easy. We have to remember what we are doing this for: because we have been extended eternal life through the sacrifice of Jesus Christ and have been commissioned to sacrificially give this opportunity to others (Matthew 28:19–20). In other words, we are not just Christian for the sake of going to Heaven but to bring as many people along with us as God gives grace to. To help those who are not so "jump-the-gun" to seek and share, here are some things to ask yourself:

1. What characteristics do I display that will attract others to follow and accept Christ as I have?

2. If I did not have a relationship with Jesus and I met someone like me, would I want to connect with them?

3. How can I share Christ in a way that makes me comfortable?

These questions will assist you in determining how you can do your part in the Christ movement on your campus. To help out a little further, let me tell you about my wife. My wife is what I like to call an "introverted extrovert". She isn't going to be the first one to jump at an opportunity to speak to someone about Jesus. At the same time, however, she won't hesitate to inform you upon inquiry that she believes in Jesus. Her method is different than mine and that is what makes her effective. I have the tendency to practically *yell* "I follow Jesus" while she just *smiles* it. She has the most inviting and welcoming smile I have ever seen (clearly considering I married her). And this is her method to share Christ. She just smiles and people are drawn to her and she finds a way to talk about Jesus. It is just that simple. Every one of us has a God-given gift or way that will draw others to Him and this is what we use to Christ the Yard.

In the previous chapter, I mentioned that there are attributes that we should pray for in order to withstand the various temptations that college will bring. The first attribute to pray for is *wisdom*. Proverbs 4:7 states that "Wisdom is the principle thing; therefore get wisdom . . . ;" which essentially means that wisdom will serve as your guide when making decisions in college. It will be very difficult at times to decide who to befriend, what groups to be a part of, and how much time you should give to extracurricular responsibilities. Wisdom will make these decisions easier.

Next we should pray for *courage*. God tells Joshua to "be strong and of good courage" three times as this young leader began the journey of his life. The same is true for you. College will be a journey, with all forms of obstacles in your path, but remember that God brought you to this place and He is with you. Courage will help you stand your ground as a Christian in the face of the opposition that you could encounter as you become vocal for Christ on your campus.

Lastly, we should pray for *resilience*. This is what this chapter is all about: standing firm for Christ when it doesn't seem like it is worth it. The Apostle Paul said it best in 1 Corinthians 15:58, "Therefore, my dear brothers and sisters, stand firm. Let nothing move you. Always give yourselves fully to the work of the Lord, because you know that your labor in the Lord is not in vain." While we pray and ask God to strengthen us during tough times, we acknowledge that we are victim to fail if we do not also seek the Holy Spirit as a guide. The Spirit will allow us to withstand certain temptations because the Spirit will detour us when necessary. Additionally, it is easier to stand when you have other people around you to keep you steadfast. Remember, in Jesus, we are a body (Ephesians 4) that requires other parts: trust your other brothers and sisters to keep you on the right path.

INTEREST QUESTIONS

1. When creating programs and desiring things that are centered on bringing other Christians together, consider your motivation. Are you trying to compete with anyone or another campus organization? Do you see your labor as worthless?

2. What is your method to reach individuals for Christ? Discuss your method with others to develop ideas and discover new ways to become comfortable with sharing your faith.

3. What are some additional attributes a person could need when attempting to spread the Gospel on the campus?

REFLECTION SCRIPTURES

- Luke 15:4–7
- Proverbs 19:21
- Matthew 28:19–20
- Proverbs 4:7
- Joshua 1:1–9
- 1 Corinthians 15:58
- Ephesians 4:1–16

Chapter Three

"Know Your Info"

Have you or someone you know ever gotten lost in your hometown? Kind of embarrassing, even if there is no other person with you, because somewhere in our mind we believe that we should just *know* where we are going because this is our birthplace. I find this to be true every time I go to Dallas to visit my family, and for some reason, especially when I bring a friend with me. Tourists always seem to want to go to a place they've heard about that you have no clue about, like "Hey man, do you know where *such and such* restaurant is? I hear they have the best *what-chamacallit*! "Now I'm forced to either pretend like I know where this newfound "tourist attraction" is, or shamefully admit I do not know. It's shameful because people expect you to know about things you are closely associated with. If you have friends like mine, you will hear something similar to this: *"Man, I thought you were from Dallas!!"* Have you ever heard a statement like this on the Yard before? It might sound a little more like this: *"Man, I thought you were a Christian!"* Statements like these will bring embarrassment and shame to any Christian when confronted with the trivial issues regarding their religious beliefs. No one wants to be categorized as a "fake" or a "poser" when it comes to who they are and what they believe. There are two ways to ensure you will hear the statement above as a believer in Christ. The first is when our actions or "walk" in Christ (I will journey further about this in the next chapter) do not agree with what others believe a Christian is supposed to be or do. The second simply boils down to this question: do we *know* about what we say we believe when we go to share with others?

I have several friends who are apart of fraternities and sororities who, to this day, being four and five years removed from college, cherish to heart the information of their respective organizations. I mean it is serious. I cannot adequately describe their commitment and loyalty to this information in words. When one of my friends meets another individual who claims to be a part of the same organization, they will challenge, or should I say interrogate, the individual with a barrage of question to determine their legitimacy. Depending on how knowledgeable the person proves to be will determine the commitment or validity of the person's claim and acceptance to who he/she declares they are. You may be thinking, "Is it really necessary to do all that?" Well, to these fraternity/sorority members, they believe in their organizations so strongly that they don't want the name of the organization to be defamed.

This is a similar mentality we should have as Christians toward God and the cause we represent, which is salvation to all by the grace given through Jesus Christ. We should desire to know all there is to know about God, Jesus, the Holy Spirit, Christianity, and the local church to ensure that our Lord is not defamed by our inability give adequate truth to those who inquire. Jesus tells the disciples in John 8:32, "you shall *know* the truth, and the truth shall make you free", implicitly stating that the continual pursuit of knowledge will give you freedom to express the truth, both inwardly and outward. The word "know" in this verse, according to Vine's Expository Dictionary of New Testament Words, is a verb that suggests that knowing is an action that should be maintained in the life of the believer. The Apostle Paul takes Jesus' words a little further in his exhortation to young Timothy when he encourages him to be diligent in his studies so there will be no room for shame because he will be able to rightly divide the word of truth (paraphrasing 2 Timothy 2:15). You see here that Paul knows the shame that can be caused when a Christian is unable to explain the truth of what we represent. To avoid discouragement, let me remind you that knowing is an ongoing process that comes by studying and testing. You won't have all the answers at every test, yet you will know what to study for when you get it wrong from time to time. Also, like a good friend, it is important to invite people to join with you in gaining new knowledge about God and the Christian faith. You can do this by inviting others to bible study, chill sessions with other Christians, and even to church. This lets others know that you desire to know the answers to their questions just as intentionally as they do.

College is the most spiritually, intellectually, and mentally stimulating place in the world. This place is filled with individuals seeking answers to questions that will define their existence, help them discover their purpose, and determine what path to take to unfold their destiny. College can be the most challenging place as well. College is also the place where a person either runs into Christ, or run away. Students are, more than anything else, seeking to discover some spiritual connection that will complete the rest of their pursuits. If we are to Christ the Yard we must be equipped with the necessary information to answer the tough questions that come from the diversity college brings to the table. There several necessary truths that a Christian must know in order to bring an individual into the "organization of Christ", but there are two that I believe are most important on the Yard.

The first truth is ***salvation is for everyone****. In the words of Emmanuel Lambert, better known as Christian Hip-Hop Artist Da T.R.U.T.H., "Jesus is for everybody."[1] Salvation is what Jesus came to offer, this is what his death ensured, and most importantly, our assurance that God desires to be in relationship with us. How do you help someone accept the salvation that comes from Jesus' salvific work on the cross? When sharing our faith, with hope that others will join us as family in the body of Christ, we must be *sincere.*

One of the most disheartening aspects of engaging others is when we are insensitive to others needs, perceptions, and understanding of our faith. We must be willing to engage others sincerely, without bias or judgement toward them. Secondly, we need to be very careful that our presentation does not appear as the "perfect saint" helping the "imperfect sinner"; in other words, establish some common ground with persons you desire to share your faith. This may seem difficult but an easy way to" break the ice" is to identify one of your weaknesses to show everyone's need for the Savior. Lastly, we must *know* what the Bible says about salvation to bring comfort to the person we are speaking with. Below are some Scriptures to help you reveal that Christ is the Savior who truly came to save the world.

1. **John 3:16-17** [16] "For God so loved the world that He gave His one and only Son that whoever believes in Him shall not perish but have eternal life. [17] For God

1. Emmanuel Lambert, *Love, Hope, War.* "JIFE"

did not send His Son into the world to condemn the world, but to save the world through Him." (TNIV)

This verse is essential when talking about Christ to others. Students want salvation, need salvation, and ultimately desire it, but often feel like they do not deserve it. Christ was sent to remove the guilt of sin so that we may be free in Him. He did not come to condemn and therefore we should not condemn others in our approach to showing salvation.

2. **Romans 10:9–10** [9] " . . . if you confess with your mouth the Lord Jesus and believe in your heart that God raised Him from the dead, you will be saved. [10] or with the heart one believes and with the mouth confession is made unto salvation." (NKJV)

3. **Romans 8:1–2** [1] "There is therefore now no condemnation to those who are in Christ Jesus, [2] because through Christ Jesus the law of the Spirit who gives life has set you free from the law of sin and death." (TNIV) This verse will eliminate the discouragement that could come from sinful acts after salvation. We are to help new believers to understand that their immediate eternal fate has changed not their ability to get everything right. Again, Jesus did not come to condemn, but to give life abundantly (John 10:10).

Remember, there are countless Scriptures that will help lead Christ to the door of the hearts of the people we are seeking to reach and as a true disciple, we should make ourselves acquainted with them.

Organizations that typically have a long, prosperous history of success are most often driven by the passion for which they were created, and the intentions of those founders of the organization. Ford Motor Company, for example, could keep a "Ford Tough" mentality when producing their vehicles because their founder, Henry Ford, was as tough as they come. Wal-Mart is the place with "Everyday Low Prices" because of founder Sam Walton's dedication to low prices and shopping convenience. Fraternities and Sororities not only ensure their members know who the founders are, but what they stood for when creating these treasured organizations. This is also a vital part of being a Christian and sharing Christ on the Yard.

The second truth to know are the ***values of our founder***. One of the main reasons people are turned away from Christians is because of their "Superficial Jesus". Shameful to say, a lot of young Christians have only a surface level relationship with Jesus that makes Him somewhat unattractive. The actual beauty of our Savior is taken away when we are unable to tell them of His unconditional **love** for all people, regardless of age, race, gender or sexual orientation, His **grace** that covers a multitude of faults, disappointments, and transgressions, and His matchless **character** that becomes visibly audible as we follow Him. Our Christian lifestyle on campus should be centered on these same values. Let's take a closer look at the "Pillars of Value" for Jesus.

1. **Love**: As we just explored with Salvation, God loved us so much that He gave us Jesus. This scripture alone should speak beyond any thought that may be fathomed about love. John also writes in 1 John 4:11–12 *"For if God so loved us, we also ought to love one another. No one has seen God at any time, if we love one another; God's love abides in us . . .*

   In other words, people should be able to experience God through our love for one another, regardless of whether they are a believer or not. Jeremiah 31:3 tells us that the love of God draws us toward God. This act that is displayed in our lives toward others when we *KNOW* our Jesus Christ as our Lord.

2. **Grace**: If someone was given the total lottery purse for only matching two of the five winning numbers, that still would not be enough grace to match what Jesus accomplished for us on the cross. Grace says that we have access to the wealth of Christ even though we don't deserve it. Examine yourself for a minute. Are there some things you don't like about yourself? God doesn't care, you are still worthy . . . THAT'S GRACE!! How easy is it to accept others and lead them to the Savior of Grace when we know how imperfect we are? In the Adventure Bible (one of the bible's infamously found in children's ministry) (NIrV), grace is described as "the kindness and forgiveness of God that is a gift and cannot be earned." That is amazing! Ephesians 2:8–9 says *"God's grace has saved you because of faith in Christ. Your salvation doesn't come from anything you do. It's a gift from God. It is not based on anything you have done. No one can brag about earning it."*

3. **Character**: The bible reveals to us the matchless character of Christ throughout the New Testament. Christ is recorded to have eaten with people whom the religious leaders considered sinners, healed those who were sick and weren't allowed into the temple, had conversations with women who prostitutes and social outcasts, and even washed his friends' feet. Who wouldn't want to get to know someone of such character! This character should be in us also. We should be compelled to get to know everyone on our Yard, befriend the person most often seen alone, chill at the table with the athletes, and engage in fellowship with the cafeteria workers. All persons are loved by God and our character in Christ should reflect how true that is.

One thing I am certain of, and that is God is inexhaustible. That's the great wonder about God. We can spend a lifetime getting to know God, the love given to us, and the matchless results following Christ will have on us and the world. However, once these truths become real in a follower's life, the world around them will change for the better, and hopefully the Yard will too!

INTEREST QUESTIONS

1. What are some creative ways you can connect with others to discuss salvation and Christ's saving power?

2. Are the values of Christ apparent in your life? What areas do you need to work on to display the values of Christ?

REFLECTION SCRIPTURES

- John 8:32
- 2 Timothy 2:15
- John 3:16–17
- Romans 10:9–10
- Romans 8:1–2
- John 10:10
- 1 John 4:11–12
- Jeremiah 31:3
- Ephesians 2:8–9

Chapter Four

Walk it Out

N ow the fun begins! When people ask me about my college experience, I often tell them that I experienced the fullness of college, except for becoming a part of a fraternity (which is one of my only regrets!). I engaged in sports, served on the Homecoming Court, ran for student government, served on several committees, traveled with organizations, engaged in missions and retreats, and even attempted to start an organization. Yet the experience I enjoyed most is becoming a Christian on the yard! I spent the first part of my college career doing everything I heard college was all about: house parties all night, taking road trips with friends to other colleges, smoking, drinking, sex, and more partying . . . I did it all! To this day, many of my friends and peers are astonished how much I've changed. I engaged the Yard with all that I had.

Therefore now, I encourage you, this is when the real fun begins. When I began to feel God tug on my heart strings in 2005, I made a commitment to be just as dedicated to sharing the goodness I felt from God as I was sharing the address to my house parties! This is also the reason I am filled with compassion and humility to engage the Yard for Christ. So, let's walk it out!

I mentioned the movie *Stomp the Yard* in the introduction because this book, in many ways, is inspired by it. In the movie, fraternities and sororities show their stuff by "stomping", or doing what is called line dances or stepping, on their college campus. During one of the scenes, the main character, DJ, engages in a dance battle with the main antagonist in the film, Grant. The song that brings this scene to life, *Walk It Out*, by Unk[1], is played while DJ humiliates Grant on the dance floor. The parallel between this scene in the movie and our commitment to Christ the Yard, minus the humiliation, of course, is to engage the campus with the genuine, uniqueness of our walk as Christians. And we should have fun doing it too!

Ephesians 4:1 encourages believers to "walk in a manner worthy of the calling to which you have been called." This means our lives should be examples that lead others into a deeper, more authentic relationship with God. Throughout much of Paul's writings, he admonishes the church to live lives that draw others. In other words, according to Paul, we do more for God with our lifestyle than we ever could with our mouth. Here are some questions you may want to consider concerning your walk:

1. Are people drawn to you because of your engagement on the Yard?

2. Do people ask you how do you "maintain" a morally compassed life while fighting the temptations of college?

3. Are you considered 'cool" by others on the campus regardless of how others view your faith in God?

1. Anthony Platt. *Walk it Out*. Atlanta, 2006

The Yard is meant to be fun. It is meant to be engaging, and inspire creativity, fellowship, and friendship. If you are a part of a Christian organization, or a Christian leader on the Yard, it is imperative that you use the creative wisdom God provides in collaboration with the activities you know will draw others to develop moments of fellowship and fun. Find commonality with others through music, culture, arts, and other things. Use your academic passions to create relationships with others that will open doors of communication and trust, that will ultimately allow for moments to share your faith in meaningful and receptive dialogue.

If you are a part of an organization, host non-Christian movies and listening sessions of music by popular mainstream artists, followed by food and discussions. Partner with non-Christian organizations to host forums to discuss current events, social issues, interfaith similarities, and other events that draw others to your understanding and perspectives on faith. These are just a few suggestions that could help engage the Yard for Christ that have the potential to create dynamic ministry and relationships.

I've been told by my friends who are members of sororities and fraternities that there is no greater feeling than when they have finished their initiation process. The elation of putting on those "letters", prancing around the Yard to let the world know of this newfound relationship. A relationship they will share with other members around the world for their entire lives. They often tell me how rewarding it is to know they are connected to people around the world through their organization, the relationships they can build with strangers who are now brothers and sisters because of this shared bond. How wonderful this must be?

As Christians, we can feel the same way. We are a part of family of brothers and sisters who share the bond of being united to God through Jesus Christ. This is the good news! Around the world is a connection to others who share the same views, dialogue over the same information (bible), trade stories of good times, bad times, challenging times, and joyous times with other brothers and sisters on our journeys on the Yard and in the world. How wonderful must this be? How wonderful it is, when brothers and sisters become bound together in God's love for the edification of one another, to reveal the nature of Christ by their walk, to give hope to the campus, and simply, graciously, with fervor and excitement . . . Christ the Yard!

INTEREST QUESTIONS

1. After reading this chapter, what events and activities are your inspired to create to build real relationships with others on the Yard?

2. What are some personal things you can change, add, or remove to make your "walk" more genuine to serve your Yard?

3. How can you walk out your faith in authentic ways on your Yard?

4. What groups are you inspired to create that will serve specific needs on your Yard after reading this chapter?

REFLECTION SCRIPTURES

- Ephesians 4:1
- Romans 1:16
- 1 Timothy 4:12
- 2 Timothy 3:16

Epilogue

The Probate

To Christian Campus Organizations:

It is my prayer this book has provided insight, wisdom, courage, and encouragement on your journey to engage your Yard for Christ. Remember the words of Paul in 1 Corinthians 3:7–9:

> So, neither the one who plants nor the one who waters is anything, but only God who gives the growth. [8] The one who plants and the one who waters have a common purpose, and each will receive wages according to the labor of each. [9] For we are God's servants, working together; you are God's field, God's building.

There are other organizations that may think about God differently, share their faith differently, and even do things you may feel are questionable from your organization's theological framework. It is my prayer that you would see them as co-labors, in the same mission field, with the same purpose, building the same Kingdom. Discover methods of communication that allow your organization to live out its purpose while discerning whether interested persons you engage would be better served in your group or another's. This allows for Christian unity on the Yard, which is one of the most effective ways to Christ the Yard.

The books recommended in the bibliography are needed to sharpen your swords, tighten your shoes, and shine your armor to be mighty and effective on your campus.

Peace and blessings!

Bibliography

Buchele, Mose. 2016. "How Did Austin Become The Live Music Capital of the World." Moody College of Communications of the University of Texas at Austin. September 21. Accessed February 1, 2017. http://kut.org/post/how-did-austin-become-live-music-capital-world.

Gonzalez, Justo. 2010. *The Story of Christianity*, Volumes 1–2. New York: HarperCollins.

Lee, Trip. 2012. *The Good Life*. Chicago: Moody Publishers.

Lutz, Stephen. 2011. College Ministry in a Post-Christian Culture. Kansas City: Beacon Hill Press.

Meeks, Wayne A. 1983. *The First Urban Christians: The Social World of the Apostle Paul*. London: Yale University Press.

Sampley, J. Paul. 1991. *Walking Between the Times*. Minneapolis: Fortress Press.

T.R.U.T.H, Da. 2013. "JIFE." *Love, Hope, War*. Cond. Emmanuel Lambert. Comp. Emmanuel Lambert.

Tabor, Corey. 2008. *Being: a 30-day Guide to Being Who God Created You to Be*. Kearney: Morris Publishing.